Shut Up, Stop Whining & Grow Your Business

7 Street Smart Strategies to Generating More Leads & Make More Profits

by Dean Renfro – Business Success Designer & Marketing Guide

COPYRIGHT AND DISCLAIMER

DEDICATION

I would like to dedicate this book to an awesome woman, my wife Lavonne. Thanks for putting up with all the ups and downs of an entrepreneurial life. To my three kids, granddaughter and grandson for living through all the trials and errors and learning failure is not a destination. And to my mentors in life, especially Dad and Mom, who lived an exemplary life of how to stay true to the course.

Dean Renfro

CONTENTS

INTRODUCTION

If you got past the cover, congratulations! This book is tough! Why? Doing business the hard way is tough! But you don't have to do business the hard, tough way. The idea in the title and some of the chapters in this book are to shake you up, make you mad! Why settle for poor lead generation, trading dollars for hours, price wars and little profits, when you don't have to? Why not just implement some tried and proven street smart strategies and practices that make your business profitable, produce as many leads as your business can handle, and position you to grow your business? Well for some it takes a kick in the butt and being ticked off to take action. For others, it's as simple as getting the hand in front of their face out of the way so they can see past the obstacles in their way. Either way, you need motivated!

While I'm making you mad, I want to make you glad. Glad that someone cares enough to get your attention, provide some options and walk you through what it takes to grow your business. Believe me, I've been where you are and I just want to give you the courage to accomplish what you want and deserve as a small business owner. A lot of business books out there are all theory! Touting things that should work or what someone wants work. You won't find any of that in this book. Some of what's in here may fly against conventional marketing theory, or what some other business owner advised, or maybe even against how 'Pops' did it!" Sometimes what works looks ugly! Sometimes getting your attention is pretty much like the mule and the two-by-four approach: you have to slap the mule between the eyes with a two-by-four to get its attention before it will do what needs to be done. Consider this book to be the two-by-four.

So read it, mark it up, and do what it says. Then celebrate!

Here's to your success,

Dean Renfro

PS. If you would like to arrange a swift kick and get a third party perspective on your business, send me an email: dean@businessprofitsacademy.com and I'll help you out!

For a pain FREE Test Drive of all my best tips, tricks and marketing resources visit http://businessprofitsacademy.com

-- Dean Renfro, Business Success Designer & Marketing Guide

1

Shut Up – Start Listening

Ok you're probably thinking, "How Rude!" Who tells a complete stranger to "shut up?" What right do I have to tell you to "shut your trap?" Well I've found that most people don't have the guts or courage to tell other people that they are rattling off at the mouth and they need to quit talking! I don't know who it was, and not quite sure if this is how they said it, but, "better to keep your mouth shut and appear a fool than open it and remove all doubt."

You see when you're talking you are not listening. Most small business owners are so busy talking that they are not paying attention! While they are talking they are missing all the important business lessons going on around them. The great sages of all ages, whether its Jesus or Jimi Hendrix all point to the fact that we need to "shush" (that's as soft as I get) and listen. As business owners we would be amazed at what we would hear and learn if we would just listen. Here's the key about listening – we usually learn something we didn't know. While talking works the other way – we're telling something we don't know!

Shush and Listen to Others

Stop talking and start listening to others, especially those closest to you - whether that's your spouse, kids, parents or close friends. Many times as business owners we are so busy with our business that when we are around others we talk about business instead of listening to those that a care about us the most. They notice things in our behavior, attitudes and demeanor. If we give them permission to talk to us about it, we might learn something about how things really are. My wife is the best listener I know. She also has the best radar I know. When she tells me something about a business or a person – I listen. When I don't it usually cost me! Quit thinking that communication is about talking, its more about listening!

Shush and Listen to Your Customers

I love what Earl Nightingale said, "All of the money you are ever going to have is currently in the hands of someone else." As a business owner you know that someone else is called a customer. Most business owners haven't studied and listened to their customer to know what makes their customer release the money in their pocket and give it to you. So start listening. Your customer (client, patient, co-worker, audience) buys when they are ready, not when you are! Learn to listen and map the buying patterns of your customer. What causes them to buy what you are selling? Do you know what problem your product, service or information solves for them? Do you know how your product, service or information makes them feel? If you been a student of listening you've probably already picked up on the fact that people usually don't buy with logic, they buy with feelings. A little side note here – you are not your customer, even if you think you are.

Shush and Listen to Your Employees

Recently I heard a local business man who is very successful and quite famous in the area say that a business owner needed to listen to his customer and his employees. Both can provide valuable information about the business. If you have employees they are your first line of representation of your business. Often they will hear or experience the good and bad of your business. It wise to keep the lines of dialogue open with them. You may have to teach them how to listen to the customer for you. You will need to have regular times of listening that are not always a formal meeting. You need honest feedback, not what they think you want to hear. You, as the owner, set the stage for that.

Shush and Listen To Those
That Know More Than You Do

First, get over yourself! You do not know everything there is to know about your business! If you think you do, you are being foolish! Someone knows more than you! It maybe only one little thing (like marketing!), but that one thing can be the difference between just getting by and becoming a million dollar company. So go find out who knows more than you. Ask them for help. One thing about our culture – if you ask for help properly, most people are glad to help! How do you ask for help? First don't whine and complain. Ask for specific help, like: "I need help generating more leads." Not, "I was kinda looking for some kinda of ideas on getting some kinda new customers, you got any?" Then when they give an answer, go do what they said! Nothing turns off a person from helping you again, than spending the time telling you how to solve your problem only to have you ignore it! Don't waste the opportunity to learn from someone who knows more than you!

Spend some time looking for, observing and listening to those that are doing better than you. Always be internally asking, "If it works for them, why not for me?" Sometimes you can just copy what they are doing and get immediate positive results. When looking for other people and businesses to model be open to businesses in industries totally unlike yours. Sometimes the best idea comes from cross-pollinating from another industry, trade or practice.

Check out my resources at http://businessprofitsacademy.com to see how to cross over ideas from different type businesses.

Shush – Listen To The Experts

Every field, every practice, every industry, every trade has its experts. Find out who they are and make it a practice to listen to them. Buy their books, their cd's, their podcast, their mp3's, and their videos. Get any of their materials offered on their websites – reports, webinars, downloads. If they travel and speak, try to attend a live event, even schedule your vacation around that opportunity. You will find that this practice alone (listening to them) will drastically improve your life and your business.

Shush – Listen To Your Self

Are you so busy talking right now that you missed what the section title is? Notice I didn't say, "yourself." What do I mean by "your self." I'm talking about your inner self. That voice deep down inside you. The one that get's passionate about what you value. The one that speaks out inside your head and heart about your moral compass. The one some people call your "gut!" Realize that your sub-conscious is working all the time in hyper mode and has gathered more information than your conscious mind can process or understand. Often times it speaks out to enlighten us, warn us, inspire us, console us and direct us. Listen and then act on what it says.

Shush – Listen To God

I would be amiss if I didn't point out to you that you are a spiritual being. And being a spiritual being implies there is a Spirit. I'm not talking about "mother earth" or the "spirit in the sky," I'm talking about God, who made us in His image, with an eternal spirit. You might not agree with me about that or you may even deny there is a God, that's your business! But if you think for a moment, that all you are is just some kind of higher animal, you need to take a deeper look at your self.

The God of Heaven speaks to us as well. He loves us, He wants the very best for us. He designed us to have a connection with Him. The problem is we don't listen to Him. Often we are listening to the other voice, the one that wants to destroy us. That voice fills us with doubt, fear, and hate. That's not God, don't listen to it. Learn to listen to God, He wrote the book on being successful and prosperous.

Shush – There's A Few You Shouldn't Listen Too

Hey, are you listening! I'm not crazy, I'm just telling you there are a few things you shouldn't listen to, okay?

Don't listen to someone who's broke tell you how to be rich!

Don't listen to a fat person tell you how to lose weight.

Don't listen to people who gossip about other people, because you'll be next.

Don't' listen to someone who has a critical spirit and a bad attitude, especially if that someone is you!

Don't listen to people who are always putting others down.

Don't listen to people who generous with the words but not with their actions.

Finally be careful with that inner voice when it turns negative, judgmental and critical. It can destroy you, your family, your business and other's around you. When you catch yourself saying negative things (I could never do that), or things that degrade you (I'm no good at that) or question your worth (I'm stupid) – STOP! Refocus, regroup and restate what you said with a positive outlook.

Wondering what all this has to do with your business? Good question! You probably already figured out that your outlook, your attitude, your vision all affect your business. If you are not willing to listen, then your employees don't listen. If you don't listen then your customer's don't listen. If they don't listen to your message and your heart, they don't buy and you don't make a sale and you will probably lose a customer and maybe your business.

So in the spirit of the chapter – SHUT UP and Listen! Got your attention again? Good cause let me prep you for the next chapter – It's real and it's ugly! So quit whining before I ever get started.

2

Stop Whining – Start Doing

It's everywhere! Everybody is doing it! What is it? Whining! Everywhere you turn people are whining! At the store, at the restaurant, at school, at work, in the break room, on TV, on the radio, at the Whitehouse, at your house, and probably in your head and maybe coming out of your mouth! Yikes! Told you it would be ugly!

Shoot we've even turned it into an entertainment factor. Can you imagine having a TV show where you bring people on stage and all they do is WHINE! There's not only one show now there are three of these and they all get high ratings! My take on that is that you've got a bunch of whiner's sitting around at home on their sofa's, watching their big screen, government bought TV, listening and watching another bunch of whiners! What a bunch of losers!

Now that you know my opinion about that, reality is that very few of us are willing to take responsibility for what is happening in our life and our business. As my friend and author Larry Wignet points out in his New York Best seller, "Shut Up, Stop Whining and Get A Life," "Why should we? No one is really asking us to." (You might guess Larry and I have similar philosophy about a few things!)

Now here's the rough part of this book – so go somewhere quiet, get alone and get ready. Are you ready? Really? Stop Whining!!!!

Every one of us is guilty of whining – complaining about everything under the sun. How it's something else, somebody else, everything else to blame for our sad, pitiful condition at the moment. It's the economy, it's the Republicans, it's the Democrats, its big oil, big business, Wall Street, China, Wal-Mart! You name it, we can blame it! – Just Stop! Stop Whining! Here's my one big take away from Larry's book:

If you are unhappy, unsuccessful, sick, or broke – it's because you want to be!

Don't do it! I'm telling you, don't do it! Don't start making excuses, blaming everybody, everything, every unseen thing! Don't do it – that's whining! Make your mind up right now; you and your business are not going to be a VICTIM! I mean it! You see the norm has become to blame something for your poor pitiful plight. You know, like your parents, you're ADHD, your birth order, breast feed or bottle feed, city born or country born. It is pathetic. Smokers want to blame tobacco companies, drunk drivers want to blame bartenders, fat people want to blame McDonalds.

Business owners are no different. We blame the marketing, the competition, economy, the customer, China, Wal-Mart, our suppliers, Government regulations, City Council, road construction, the weather, the internet, you name it! It's everybody else's fault but ours. We are innocent! Our whole nation is turning into a nation of whiners and blamers. How sad.

Stop Whining – It Is Your Fault

That probably just went over like a lead balloon! I mean, cut some slack here right? NOT! I know your business is different that everybody else's, right? Really? You honestly expect me to believe that you are that naïve? If you think your business is totally different than everyone else's, you just discovered one of your problems! It's not! Yes, maybe the widget is different, maybe the technology is different, maybe the process is different. But in the end it works and functions like every business. So as my dad says, "Fix your stinkin' thinkin." One of the major reasons businesses struggle is because they somehow think they are unique and different from every other business, therefore there is some secret magic formula that has to be discovered to make it work. Really?

Another reason you need to stop whining and admit it's your fault – you are not willing to do what it takes for your business to be successful. I see it all the time. The other day in an empty barber shop in the middle of the afternoon a barber tells me, I'm doing fine. I really don't want any more business. You know what? He's going to get exactly what he wants. Most business owners are just not willing to do what it takes to grow their business to the next level. They are comfortable right where they are at. What you don't realize is that a day is coming and it's right around the corner, and puff! All your business is gone. They are fat and satisfied. My granddad had another word for that – lazy!

The third reason it's your fault – you don't care. Or as my neighbor says, "You don't give a damn." I know this is a hard pill to swallow. I mean, it is for me. But when I look out or look deep within and realize that I could do better, I can be smarter, I can care more – then I realize that the reason I'm not being better, smarter or caring – is because deep down – I don't care. I'll be the first to admit and have, "I can do more." Question is, "Can You?" "Will You?"

You see as a business owner its success or lack thereof, really is in your hands. If you have been in business any time at all, you have probably experience all the above with someone or some other business. Being plain stupid about something, or just being lazy and not trying, or just not caring. How did you feel? Like totally disgusted? Like – they don't deserve to be in business? Be careful here – that might be your business you're seeing.

Stop Whining – Stuff Happens

Look stuff happens – you know it, I know it. It doesn't matter where we are from and where we are going – stuff happens. To quote the Bible – "It rains on the just and the unjust." Stop and think about it, if "stuff" didn't happen, life would be boring. Business would be boring. Matter of fact most of us wouldn't even be in business because our business exist because "stuff happens" and we have the answer or solutions to someone else's "stuff."

Your business is where it is because of the choice you made or failed to make. You got loyal customers or you don't, but it's on you. You make a good profit or not, but it's on you. You trade dollars for hours or not, but it's on you. Your employees respect you or not, but it's on you. Had enough? Not yet – one more thing.

I know from personal business experience, materials don't show up, people quit at the most inopportune moments, customer's checks bounce, and people lie. You know this too! To quote Larry again, "Few people will turn

14

to themselves to take responsibility for their results until they have exhausted all opportunities to blame someone else."

Here's your one thing – there is no "Get Out Of Jail Free" card for making bad choices or being stupid. The government is not going to rescue you, buy you cell phone, put gas in your car, save your home. They might say they are, but they're not. Superman is not going to sweep down and rescue you from your dumb mistakes (intentional or accidental). Stop Whining – Start Doing!

Start Doing What?

Actually it's pretty simple (actually most things are). You have two choices, focus on whining or focus on solving the problem. You can only choose one! So, start cleaning up your own messes. Fix your own problems. Pay your own bills. Admit your own mistakes. Start investing in your customer, your employees, your business. Start taking control; quit being a victim of circumstance. I know things happen outside our control. But, I am still in charge of my reaction to that circumstance. I still can choose how to respond. Choose to be responsible and not whine!

Man, I bet you're glad this chapter is over. (Quit whining!) Figured out its time to stop whining? Stopped making excuses? Okay now that we're listening and taking responsibility, I think we're ready to really grow our business, generate more leads and make more money! You ready? That's what's next – seven street smart strategies that can help you explode your business. But here's the key – You have to Do It! All I can do is give you a map!

3

Define Your Target Market
Street Smart Strategy #1

I know you might already be tempted to whine, but this first strategy is really important. You get this wrong and you lose your business! Countless businesses have made major errors in this one area alone. So pay attention and do the exercises and listen to others about this key strategy.

What is a Target Market?

Many businesses can't answer the question: *Who is your target market?* They have often made the fatal assumption that *everyone* will want to purchase their product or service with the right marketing strategy.

A target market is simply the group of customers or clients who will purchase a specific product or service. This group of people all have something in common, often age, gender, hobbies, or location.

Your target market, then, are the people who will buy your offering. This includes both existing and potential customers, all of whom are motivated to do one of three things:

- Fulfill a need
- Solve a problem

- Satisfy a desire

To build, maintain, and grow your business, you need to know who your customers are, what they do, what they like, and why they would buy your product or service. Getting this wrong – or not taking the time to get it right – will cost you time, money, and potentially the success of your business.

The Importance of Knowing Your Target Market

Knowledge and understanding of your target market is the keystone in the arch of your business. Without it, your product or service positioning, pricing, marketing strategy, and eventually, your business could very quickly fall apart.

If you don't intimately know your target market, you run the risk of making mistakes when it comes to establishing pricing, product mix, or service packages. Your marketing strategy will lack direction, and produce mediocre results at best. Even if your marketing message and unique selling proposition (USP) are clear, and your brochure is perfectly designed, it means nothing unless it arrives in the hands (or ears) of the right people.

Determining your target market takes time and careful diligence. While it often starts with a best guess, assumptions cannot be relied on and research is required to confirm original ideas. Your target market is not always your ideal market.

Once you build an understanding of who your target market is, keep up with your market research. Having your finger on the pulse of their motivations and drivers – which naturally change – will help you to anticipate needs or wants and evolve your business.

So, if we met on the street tomorrow and I asked you, "Who's your customer?" Could you tell me? I mean could you rattle off all the things in this chapter so that I would immediately know, you know your customer? If you can, great! If you can't, work on it until you get it. If you have employees, even if it's just one, you need to have a debriefing period with them and paint the picture of your ideal target market. Make sure they understand the target market. I want to offer you a free resource that can help you determine your target market, got to http://businessprofitsacademy.com/myguidedtour and sign up for the free four part video series. Our team will help you identify how you can get started generating all the leads your business can handle.

Another reason you need to know your ideal target market is so that when you see it, you can take action. Which is what I'm going to talk about in the next chapter.

4

Create Added Value in Your Business and Make 1 + 1 = 3
Street Smart Strategy #2

Next to knowing your target market, this component is key in creating life-long customers. As you learn to listen to your target market, observe trends in your target market, create solutions for your target market this key behavior will emerge as your secret weapon. What you have to learn here is "value in = value out." Most business owners don't get this. For them it's all about the sale. Don't miss this huge key of creating an irresistible reason for your target market to do business with you and only you. Here's how.

The majority of small businesses, like yours, are established in response to market demand for a product or service. Many build their businesses by serving that demand, and enjoy growing profits without putting much effort into long-term planning or marketing.

However, what happens when that demand slows or stops? What happens when the competition sets up shop with a "new and improved" version of your product down the road? How do you keep your offering fresh, while growing and maintaining your client base? The answer is by adding value to your product or service.

Added value is a marketing or customer relations strategy that can take the form of a product, service, which is added to the original offering for free, or as part of a discounted package. It, like all other elements in your marketing toolkit, is designed to attract new customers and retain existing ones. A simple example of added value would be if you owned a gift shop, and offered complimentary gift wrapping with every purchase.

If you don't refresh and renew your offering over time, your customers will get bored and be drawn to your competitor. Your employees, too, may become disinterested, and find work elsewhere. Ultimately, both clients and employees will demand additional value to remain loyal – and aren't they the keystones for your business growth?

Can You Add Value to Your Business?

Everyone can add value to their business. Better yet, everyone can *afford* to add value to their business. Adding value doesn't have to blow your marketing budget, or take up hours of your time. There are many ways – big and small – to enhance your business in the eyes of your clients.

The key to adding value is determining what your customers and target market perceive as valuable. You must understand their needs, wants, troubles and inconveniences in order to entice them with solutions through added value products or services. Adding value will add to your profits, but if you don't focus on genuinely helping your clients, you'll have a difficult time attracting them.

Added value works for both product- and service-based businesses. If you offer a service, like hairstyling, try treating your customers with products like a latte while they wait, shampoo samples, or a free conditioning treatment with every sixth visit. If you sell a product, consider offering convenience services – like free shipping or delivery – to make the customer's experience a seamless one. The customer will feel appreciated and their needs will have been taken care of.

Ways to Add Value to Your Business

There are many ways to enhance your offer, depending on your budget and the resources you have access to. You may wish to hold a brainstorming session with your staff to come up with ideas for your business; if your employees are on the front lines, they'll likely have firsthand information about what clients would like to see more of. Here's a few ideas to get you started

Feature Your Expertise

Your intellectual property is a free resource that you have at your disposal to share with your clients. This will make them feel as though they have an inside track. You might want to consider adding it to your business, making it a value-added service.

Expert corner: Supplement your website and newsletter with columns on topics of interest to your customers and of relevance to your service. This will position you as an expert in the marketplace, and give your clients helpful information they won't receive from the competition.

Do It Yourself Tips: This is a great tool for seasonal marketing. Provide your clients with this information on your website, in your newsletters, or on take away note cards in your store or office. Ideas include recipes, craft ideas, gift ideas – all of which are branded with your company logo and contact information, and include your product as an ingredient.

Offer Convenience Services

Customer service is a dying practice in our high paced culture – use it to your advantage. When done well, it can be the difference between you and the competition, or the deciding factor for a potential repeat client.

Envision the steps involved for a customer to arrive at your store, purchase your offering, and use your product or service. Can you eliminate any of those steps for them? Can you shorten waiting times, or make them more pleasurable? Stepping into your clients' shoes will allow you to determine the most powerful value add for your company. Here are a few ideas:

Free Delivery + Shipping
Follow up Services
Gift-Wrapping
"While You Wait" Amenities
Comparison-Shopping Tools

Establish Complementary Partnerships

Complementary partnerships with other businesses can take you a long way toward adding value for your customer, and generating new business. Just like a joint testimonial mailing, the power (and convenience) of referral business is immense.

Build a web of associates.

Establish partnerships with financial incentives **Location-based partnerships**

Packages + Bundles

Packaging and bundling products and services is one of the most popular methods of adding value. Clients perceive the bundles as having a higher value than the sum of the individual items – or as receiving something for free.

Cleverly packaged and named bundles can spark interest and revive your products in the eyes of your customers. Remember to always give the offers an end date or provide a limited number to create a sense of scarcity and urgency and to prevent this strategy from going stale.

Intuitive product bundles
Package your upsell

Offer a Customer Loyalty Program

There are a number of ways to structure your rewards and loyalty program, depending on the type of business and level of technological resources available to you. Customer loyalty programs have a huge advantage – they help build your database of customer information and in most cases allow you to view and analyze purchasing patterns. Here are the most popular:

Every 6th (or 10th) Visit on Us
Rewards Dollars
Rewards Points
Membership Amenities

Look, business doing what you do, or selling what you sell abound. There are very few businesses with a unique product or service. If you stay inside the norm you will wind up competing on price. In my opinion that's for businesses that want to go broke or spend years in misery trying to hold on and survive. That's why you got in business, right? To just survive?

Refuse to get into a price war! Refuse to be just like everybody else, except with at twist! Decide to create such a huge value in your business that your customers are going to do business with you no matter the cost, because that is not the issue. You see, if you create "value alignment" you'll be amazed by all the things customers will do and put up with to do business with you.

Recently a franchise chain had a big promotion day that fans of that chain from all across the country flooded their stores to purchase their products. I personally witnessed hundreds and hundreds of people stand in line for over an hour at a time to buy a $3.50 sandwich! While another national chain right next door who also sells a similar product was nearly empty most of the day. This particular store set a record for sales in one day (it was in the seven figures). Why? Value Alignment! What that store and company stood for lined up with the values of its customers. I personally stood on a chair at that store for eight hours calling out people's orders, all for free! Why? Value-Alignment! Don't underestimate the power of value alignment. Find out what alignment you can create with your target market and create the value, practice it, talk about, demonstrate it and watch what happens.

Just like creating a huge value component to your business and discovering the power of value alignment, you also must learn the same power of marketing alignment. That's the next street smart strategy you need to master.

5

Creating Effective Marketing Material
Street Smart Strategy #3

A street smart business has to be aware of its surroundings and how it shows itself to its market. Many times businesses owners get enamored with "shiny objects." They see one business is using this marketing piece, so they copy the same thing – only to be disappointed with no or little results. Then they see another business is doing social media, so they rush to create a Facebook page or Twitter, or Linked-In, or Google + page. Nothing happens – disappointed again. Suddenly "marketing" becomes the bad guy. Marketing get's blamed for all the poor results. Here's what you need to know – you have to create marketing alignment.

Your marketing collateral gets sent out in the world to do one thing: act as an ambassador for your product or service, in place of *you*. This may seem like a big job for a piece of paper, but it's a helpful way to think about the materials you create.

When you meet with a potential or existing client, you do a number of things. You make sure you are well prepared with all the information the customer could need. You dress in clothing that is appropriate. You anticipate their needs, and offer a solution to their problems. You may also cater to how they best like to receive information.

Chances are, you wouldn't meet with clients just for the sake of meeting with a client – say, for instance, to show off your new suit. Likewise, you shouldn't create and distribute collateral that is non-essential.

We all know that the biggest challenge for small businesses is the limited number of zeros attached to their marketing budget. Marketing materials can be expensive, and a single, well-produced piece has the ability to devour the entire budget. Given that billion-dollar marketing campaigns fail every day, how can you be sure to make the most of, and be successful with, the dollars you're working within?

The answer? Limit yourself to only the essential items for your individual business, and produce them *well* with the resources you have. Marketing is built around a message, your message. Great graphics is important. A logo for brand identification is important. Catchy slogans are important. But remember you only have one chance to capture someone's attention and create a memorable impression. Be wise!

Your Essential Marketing Materials

The easiest way to throw away your marketing budget is to create and produce marketing materials *you don't need*. Since many pieces of collateral are paper-based, this not only leaves you with boxes of extra (outdated) materials, but also takes a huge toll on the environment.

Take some time to determine what marketing materials you do need, and stick to your list. It's easy to want to "keep up with the Joneses" when your competition comes out with a new piece, but remember your focus should be on attracting and retaining a customer base, not matching the competition item for item.

Know your target market. Make sure you have a solid understanding of your customer base. From that knowledge, you can easily determine what the best way is to reach out and communicate with them. Are they a paper-based or techno savvy client group? Do they appreciate being contacted by email or mail? Are they impressed by flashy design, or simple pieces? *How* you communicate is often just as or more important than *what* you communicate.

Pay attention to costs. Do you really need a die-cut business card? Does your flyer absolutely require ink to the edges? Unique touches to marketing collateral can grab a customer's attention, but they can also dramatically increase the cost of production. Keep an eye out during the design process and make strategic choices about graphic elements.

Make mistakes – in small batches. Not sure if that flyer is going to do the trick? Testing out a limited time offer? Small production runs may cost a little more, but you'll avoid collecting boxes of unusable materials. Or, try a split run with type versions of the same piece and see what works best.

Keep the environment in mind. Environmental responsibility is on everyone's mind these days – including your customers. Always question if a particular marketing item can be produced in electronic format. Consider eliminating plastic bags in exchange for cloth ones, printed with your logo; print everything double-sided; send electronic newsletters; use your website to communicate; and, use recycled paper and envelopes when you can.

Brainstorm your wish list. Create a list of desired marketing materials, and ignore expenses, clients, or any other constraint. Then, beside each item, indicate realistically if it is a needed, wanted, not needed, or electronic item. The next page includes a checklist to get you started. Once you have finished, re-write your list in priority order. This will keep you focused on the essentials only.

Marketing Materials Checklist

Item	Need	Want	Don't Need	Electronic
Logo				
Business Cards				
Brochure				
Website				
Newsletter				
Catalogue				
Advertisements				
Flyers				
Fridge Magnet				
Branded Swag (pens, etc.)				
Employee Clothing				
Product Labels				
Signage				
Internal Templates (Fax Cover, Memo, etc.)				
Email Signature				
Blog				
Letterhead + Envelopes				
Thank You Cards				
Notepads				
Seasonal Gifts				
Company Profile				

At Business Profits Academy, we not only teach and train about marketing we also provide it. Our unique system allows us to create a turnkey marketing package, all the way from a receptionist's telephone script to a full blown TV commercial and everything in between.

The aspect of all your marketing materials is to lead your potential customer into your sales funnel. Whether the funnel a simple straight-line process or an elaborate grid of options you want all your material focused on getting them in at some entry point. Your ability to measure your marketing material is also important. If you can't measure it, why would you do it? Often business spend enormous amounts on marketing without being able to quantify the results. As a small business owner you can't afford that luxury. Measure it, track it, evaluate it so you can modify it, repeat it or delete it.

Once you have your marketing materials working for you the next process is to begin to leverage it to create more leads and grow your profits. By leveraging and positioning your marketing you can often create income streams from unseemly places.

6

Profits from Fresh Air
Street Smart Strategy #4

As a small business owner, you are in business for one reason: to make money. Business owners argue this all the time. Many times they have been seduced into thinking that "making money" as their primary reason for existence is "evil." Wake UP!

If you don't make money you won't be in business very long. I don't care how noble a cause, how much of a humanitarian you are, you can only go as far as your money will take you. Simple formula: NO MONEY – NO BUSINESS. Now that we are clear on that, take a deep breath.

Of course, there are other reasons you started or purchased your company. You may love the product you sell, or service you provide. You may love the challenge of turning a floundering company into an overnight success. You may just love being your own boss.

Naturally, this all means nothing if you are not generating enough income to support yourself and your family, as well as the people who work for you.

Nearly all businesses make money. Unless not a single product or service is sold, there is always money coming in. But there is also always money going out. Supplies, wages, marketing, acquisitions and operations all contribute to the expense of just staying in business.

Simply put, profit is the difference between money in and money out. This is the dollar value of your sales, minus the cost of those sales.

In business, you will find that everyone wants to make more money. They want to increase their sales, get more money coming in. **What often gets overlooked is that the true secret to making more money is not increasing sales, but increasing profit.**

The Basics of Increasing Profit

Your Profitability Goal

Now that you have an understanding of the current profitability of your company, it is time to look at ways to increase your bottom line.

Like all other aspects of your business development, you need to have a clear idea of your intention or purpose before you begin any activity. Assuming you wish to increase the profitability of your business, you need to determine by how much and within what time frame.

Create a profit-related goal for your business, and write it here:

_____

Three Ways to Increase Profit

There are countless strategies for increasing profit, but ultimately you can only increase profit in one of three ways:

1. Get More Customers

Use marketing outreach strategies to generate more leads, and convert those leads into more customers. Introduce a new offer, expand your target audience, or approach a new target audience.

2. Get Your Customers to Buy More Often

Use customer loyalty and retention strategies to get your existing customers to buy from you more often. Make it easy for them to come back and do business with you.

You can do this by adding value to your product or service, keeping in touch on a regular basis, and giving your customers incentive to make repeat purchases. Customer service is also an overlooked component of building a repeat client base.

3. Increase How Much Your Customers Buy

You'll naturally increase your sales when you increase the number of customers and how often they purchase. The final way you can impact your profit is by increasing the average dollar value of each sale.

This can be achieved by up-selling every customer, creating package offers, and finding ways to increase the perceived value of your offering to justify increasing the price.

Strategies to Increase Profit

Once you have a concrete understanding of where your business stands today in terms of profitability, minimized your operating costs, and restructured your pricing strategy, you can focus on other strategies to increase profit.

There are countless strategies and tactics that will help you to bring in more customers, get those customers to come back, and get those customers to spend more when they do.

Here is a list of ideas, many of which are covered in detail in other sections of this program:

- Advertise
- Establish an online presence
- Sell more high margin items
- Generate more leads
- Focus on referral business
- Increase customer loyalty and repeat business
- Increase conversion rates
- Restructure your team
- Reinvent your product
- Sell your intellectual capital

Understanding your price spread, profit margins, price elasticity, and money movement are key to you breaking even, or worse going broke, and making profit. If you don't track this process it can sneak up on you and surprise you. Often business owners are so busy running the business that they miss the sign post of sliding profits. Creating profit road map must be a huge priority. Once you position your profit strategy you are ready to flood your business with customers.

7

Generating an Unlimited Amount of Leads for Your Business
Street Smart Strategy #5

I am totally amazed by the all the business owners who have bought into the "field of dreams" philosophy. You know, "Build it and they will come." Everyday all across America people invest their lives into a "hope so" approach. They open doors and hope someone shows up. They put up signs and hope someone will see it and do business with them.

Want to test this? Walk into just about any business and ask, "How many sales will you make today/" Almost always the answer is going to be, "It all depends on how many customer's show up." What that means is, they have no idea how many sales they are going to make because they are hoping someone shows up. One of the most hilarious approaches to testing this concept is when an "ads" salesperson approaches you is to agree to their ad piece but tell you will pay them when enough leads come in from the ad to support the payment for the ad. Get ready for some dirty looks, maybe even some dirty words! These tactics along with countless others have totally sucked a business owner dry when they miss this key question: Where do your customers come from?

Most people would probably choose advertising as an answer. Or referrals. Or direct mail campaigns. This may seem true, but it's not really accurate.

Your customers come from leads that have been turned into sales. Each customer goes through a two-step process before they arrive with their wallets open. They have been converted from a member of a target market, to a lead, then to a customer.

So, would it not stand to reason then, that when you advertise or send any marketing material out to your target market, that you're not really trying to generate customers? That instead, you're trying to generate leads.

When you look at your marketing campaign from this perspective, the idea of generating leads as compared to customers seems a lot less daunting. The pressure of closing sales is no longer placed on advertisements or brochures.

From this perspective, the **general purpose of your advertising and marketing efforts is then to generate leads from qualified customers.** Seems easy enough, doesn't it?
We've created a lead generation system that will help you generate all the lead your business can handle. Check out my free resource that teaches you how to do exactly that:

     http://businessprofitsacademy.com/myguidedtour

You probably figured out that the key to leads is to have a system. A system to find leads, a system to get leads into a funnel, a system to get referrals from the leads, and a system to follow up the leads and one to nurture the leads over a time and keep them buying again. Which leads us to the   next   street   smart   strategy.

8

How to Create Repeat Business and Have Clients that Pay, Stay and Refer
Street Smart Strategy #6

One of the greatest profit generators lies in this often overlooked area – repeat customer business. Often because of the hurriedness of business life, small business owners don't give a lot of thought to how to create a continuity of business with their existing customers. The assumption is, "You like me or my product, therefore you'll come back and buy from me." Bad assumption!

This happens in every industry, doctors, dentist, restaurants, you name it, we are all guilty. How you view this concept will determine your ability to create customer continuity – "Do I get customers to be able to make a sale? Or Do I make sales to get customers? This is a key question that I learned from Dan Kennedy, author of the "NO B.S." series of books on marketing. Your answer to that question is key. Here's why.

When it comes to marketing and generating more income, most business owners are focused outward.

They've carefully established and segmented their target market, and created specific offers and messages for each market segment. They spend thousands of dollars in advertising and direct mail campaigns in hot pursuit of more leads, more customers, and more foot traffic.

While this is an effective way to build a business, it is costly and time consuming. It requires constant and consistent effort, and while this approach does generate results, those results quickly disappear when the effort stops or becomes less intense.

Successful businesses that see sustained growth have a double-edged marketing strategy. They focus their efforts *outward* – on new potential customers and marketing – as well as *inward* – on existing customers and referral business.

These successful businesses have leveraged their existing efforts to generate more revenue. Simply put, their customers buy from them over and over again.

For most businesses, this is the easiest way to increase their revenues. Simple customer loyalty strategies and outstanding customer service are often all you need to dramatically increase your sales – from the customers you already have.

The Cost of Your Customers

Do you know how much it costs your business to buy new customers?

Each new customer that walks through your door – with the exception of referrals – has cost you money to acquire. You have spent money on advertising and promotions to generate leads and turn those leads into customers.

For example, if you have placed an ad in your local newspaper for $1,000, and the ad brings in 10 customers, you have paid $100 to acquire each customer. You would need to ensure each of those customers spent at least $200 to cover your margin and break even.

Alternately, if you spent two hours of your time and $10 per month on an email marketing program to send a newsletter to your existing database of customers, and you bring in 10 customers as a result – each customer has cost you $1.

Generating more repeat business means focusing on the marketing strategies that aim to keep your existing customers instead of purchase new ones – effectively reducing the cost of attracting new customers to your business.

These strategies are simple to implement, and don't require much time investment. Just a solid understanding of how to make customers want to come back and spend more of their money

Keeping Your Customers

Marketing strategies that focus on keeping your current customer base are easy and enjoyable to implement. They allow you to build real relationships with the people you do business with, instead of dealing with a revolving door of people on the other end of your sales process.

Repeat customers create a community of people around your business that presumably share the same needs, desires and frustrations. The information you gain from these customers (market research) can help you strengthen your understanding of your target audience, and more accurately segment it.

Remember – 80% of your revenue comes from 20% of your customers. Always focus on these customers. They are ideal customers that you want to recruit, and hold on to.

Customer Service: Make them love buying from you

Every business – even those with excellent service standards can improve the service they provide their customers. Customer service seems to be a dying concept in most businesses; more focus seems to be placed on the speed of the transaction. These days you can even go to the grocery store now and not speak to a single sales associate thanks to self-serve checkouts.

To improve your company's customer service standards, take a survey of your customers and your employees to brainstorm ways you can improve the experience of buying from your business.

Successful customer service standards – those that make your customers *buy* – are:

Consistent. The standards are up kept by every person in your organization. Expectations are clear and followed through. Customers know what to expect, and choose your business because of those expectations.

Convenient. It is nearly effortless for the customer to spend money at your place of business. Convenience can take many forms – location, product selection, value-added services like delivery – and it is also consistent.

Customer-driven. The service the customer receives is exactly how they would like to be treated when buying your product or service. It is reflective of your target market, and appropriate to their lifestyle. Customers would probably not appreciate white linen tablecloths at a fast food restaurant, but they would appreciate a 2-minutes or less guarantee.

Newsletters: Keep in touch with your customers

A regular newsletter is an easy, time-effective, and inexpensive marketing strategy to implement. Unfortunately, many small businesses think these are too time consuming and too expensive to adopt as part of their marketing strategy.

The most popular type of newsletter distribution is email. This will cost your business as little at $10 per month for an email marketing service subscription, and can be customized to your unique branding.

Here is an easy five-step process to starting a company newsletter:

1. Pick your audience. New customers? Market segment? Existing customers?

2. Choose what you're going to say. Company news? Feature product? New offer?

3. Determine how you're going to say it. Articles? Bullet points? Pictures?

4. Decide how it's going to get to your audience. Email? Mail? In-store?

5. Track your results. How many people opened it? Read it? Took action?

Value Added Service: Give them happy surprises

Adding value to your business is an effective way of getting your customers back. Every person I know would choose a mattress store that offered free delivery over one that did not. It's that simple.

There are many ways to add value to your business, including:

o   **Feature your expertise.** Use your knowledge to provide additional value to your customers. Offer a free consumer guide or report with every purchase.

o   **Add convenience services.** Offer a service that makes their purchase easier, or more convenient. The best example of this is free shipping or delivery.

o   **Package complementary services**. Packaging like items together creates an increase in perceived value. This is great for start-up kits.

o **Offer new products or services**. Feature top of the line or exclusive products, available only at your business. Offer a new service or profile a new staff member with niche expertise.

Value added services generate repeat customers in one of two ways:

1. Impress them on their first visit. Impress you customer with great service, a product that meets their needs, and then wow them with something extra that they weren't expecting. Get them to associate the experience of dealing with your business with happy surprises, and create a perception of higher value.

2. Entice them to come back. The introduction of a new value-added service can be enough to convince a customer to buy from you again. Their initial purchase established a trust and knowledge of your business and its processes. They will want to "be included" in anything new you have to offer – especially if there is exclusivity. It is easier to attract clients that have purchased from you than potential clients who have not.

Customer Loyalty Programs: Give them incentives

Another simple way to keep in touch with existing customers and keep them coming back to you is to create a customer loyalty program.

These programs do not have to be complicated or costly, and are relatively easy to maintain once they have been implemented. These programs help you gain more information on your customers and their purchasing habits.

Here are some examples of simple loyalty programs that you can implement:

Free product or service. Give them every 10th (or 6th) product or service free. Produce stamp cards with your logo and contact information on it.

Reward dollars. Give them a certain percentage of their purchase back in money that can only be spent in-store. Produce "funny money" with your logo and brand.

Rewards points. Give them a certain number of points for every dollar they spend. These points can be spent in-store, or on special items you bring in for points only.

Membership amenities. Give members access to VIP amenities that are not available to other customers. Produce member cards or give out member numbers.

Hopefully you grasped the importance of making a sale to gain a customer. This key is the portal to creating wealth a with your customers. Remember that in order for this strategy to work, you and your team have to understand and promote it. The program in itself becomes a product that you sell.

Another necessary component of the system and the ability to create a profitable business is developing a mindset and process that generates from every piece of promotion, advertisement, sales copy, signage, even your business card the ability to have a direct response. You must be able to measure the effectiveness of everything you do. The next street smart strategy thought to be dead by many is one of the most cost effective and easiest to measure forms of direct response you can invest in.

9

How to Profit from Direct Mail
Street Smart Strategy #7

Don't believe the lie that direct mail is dead! It's totally inaccurate. The largest internet search engine in the world uses direct mail to interact with customers! Done correctly with the right process that interrupts, engages, educates and then calls the reader to take action is the best use of a business's time, energy and money. Every time you mail an existing or potential customer a letter, send an email, post a message and ask them to respond or take action, you are running a direct-mail campaign.

Direct mail is a marketing strategy that can help you achieve a number of business objectives. From lead generation to customer retention, direct mail campaigns are a highly versatile and relatively cost-effective choice for business promotion.

What you probably don't realize is that direct mail is one of the most targeted marketing strategies you can implement, and one of the easiest to track, measure and analyze results.

It is also one of the most personal. Instead of an advertisement, flyer, newspaper insert or catalogue, you are sending each customer a personalized letter that is tailored to their unique needs and desires.

Getting the most out of your direct mail campaign is easy. With a laser-sharp mailing list and irresistible offer, your direct mail campaign can easily flood your business with qualified leads.

Let's get started!

A List of Ideal Customers

Unless you spend time carefully crafting a mailing list of ideal customers, you may as well pack and up go home. The success of a direct mail campaign largely rests on the pinpoint accuracy of your mailing list.

The only people you want on your list are your potential "ideal customers." The people who are most likely to buy from you – often and in large volumes – and who are a delight to deal with. They are the type of people who will account for 80% of your revenue, and just 20% of your total customer base.

You have a number of options when you are creating your mailing list:

- **Existing customer database**. This is a list of all of the people who have previously purchased from you. It is important to gather their full contact information at the time of sale so you will be able to get contact them again.

- **Existing leads database**. This is a list of all of the leads that have come through your door, but have not purchased from you. This may include those who responded to your last direct mail campaign, but have not yet become customers.

- **Outsourced list**. This is a list that has been purchased from a market research firm, the government, or the post office. These lists are pulled based on demographic information – age, sex, location, income, family structure, etc.

Putting the mailing list together

Once you have determined the source(s) for your mailing list, you will have to spend some time assembling it and preparing it for your mailing.

1. Make sure all contacts are up to date. Phone old contacts to confirm their mailing address. An out-of-date list will cost you money in printing and postage.

2. Ensure all contacts are accurate to the list criteria. Take a read through your list to make sure there are no contacts that shouldn't be on the list.

3. Use a database management program to manage your mailing. This will allow you to keep a master list, and create custom lists for each mailing. Remember to save the file name as something that describes the mailing so you can easily find it.

Writing Effective Direct Mail Pieces

Now that you have a laser-sharp mailing list, you will want to do everything you can to target your message to the recipients on your list.

An effective direct mail piece:

- **Has a clear structure.** The piece is clearly a letter – there is an engaging headline, clear message, point form list of benefits, and postscript.

- **Features an irresistible offer.** The purchase opportunity is too good for the target audience to refuse. It includes an element of scarcity and urgency.

- **Focuses on customer benefits.** The customer clearly understands "what's in it for me?" The product or service is clearly positioned as something of value and a solution to a need, problem, or desire.

- **Is personal and conversational.** The letter is personally addressed, and reads as though it was composed specifically for the recipient. It is written in conversational tone, with short sentences and limited description.

- **Is short.** The letter communicates what it needs to, and closes. It does not go on for pages in length. The messages are clear, succinct, and simple.

- **Is urgent.** The piece gives the reader to act immediately. There is a time limit or a quantity limit to the offer that requires an urgent response.

- **Includes a Postscript.** The offer or urgency is repeated after the signature at the bottom of the letter. Like a headline, everyone will read the P.S.

The Five-Step Direct Mail Campaign

1. Determine Your Target Audience

As we discussed above, you will want to ensure that you have the most accurate, targeted list possible for your direct mail campaign.

Be clear about the purpose for your direct mail campaign – this will help you decide if you want to send your letters to your entire target market, a segment of that market, existing customers, or potentially a referring business's customers. Then you can determine how you craft your offer, how you structure your letter, and when you choose to send it.

2. Choose what you want to say

What is the message you want to communicate to your target list? What can you offer them that will entice them to act immediately?

Create a specific offer for each direct mail campaign to ensure each time you communicate with your target list you have something new to say. Tailor this offer to each mailing list.

Decide what product or service benefits will be most compelling to your target audience, and include those benefits prominently in your letter.

3. Develop a compelling direct mail piece

You are in control of how your format your message. Are you sending a letter? A brochure and a letter? A postcard? The format of your direct mail piece needs to be tailored to your target list, and reflect your product or service. A younger audience may respond to a postcard, but an older audience may appreciate a formalized letter.

Ensure that whatever format you choose, the piece is professionally designed, prominently includes your logo and company branding, and is professionally produced.

This piece of paper has to act as an ambassador of your company – you absolutely need it to appear impressive and professional.

4. Pick your timing

Some products and purchase decisions are best made at certain times of the year, or the month. If your business or service is seasonal, then there are good times and bad times to try to generate leads. Consider the best purchase windows for the people in your target marketing. When do they get paid? When do they have the money to spend on your product/service? When do they spend the most money?

Anticipate these windows, and time your direct mail campaign accordingly. If you run a lawn sprinkler installation system and summer is your peak season, run a direct mail campaign mid-way through spring, and at the beginning of summer.

Some common time windows include:

- Holiday season (November – December)
- Fridays (paydays)
- The 15th and 30th of every months (also paydays)
- Seasons (Spring, Summer, Fall, Winter)
- Financial cycles (year-end, tax time)
- Sports seasons (hockey, football, baseball, etc.)

5. Follow up

Comprehensive follow up to a direct mail campaign means two things:

1. **Following up on your letter with a phone call or second letter**
   Often it takes more than a letter to get a potential customer to take action. This can be a result of the accuracy of your mailing list, your offer, the time of the year, or the quality of the marketing material (brochure). If you are certain that your mailing list is accurate and up to date, follow up to the piece with a phone call, or send another letter, postcard, email, or personal visit. The key is to follow up, follow up, follow up!

2. **Recording, measuring and analyzing your results.**

   It is essential that you evaluate each direct mail campaign based on your time and financial investment and your rate of response. How else will you be able to tell if it was a successful or effective strategy?

For each campaign, record and analyze the following information:

- Number of letters sent
- Number or responses as a percentage
- Number of sales directly resulting from the campaign
- Number of enquiries
- Total value of sales directly resulting from the campaign

Based on this information, determine if the campaign was successful (did it make you money?) or not. Consider making some changes to your list, your offer, or the piece itself, and try again.

There are three choices when it comes to direct marketing. You can look around and see what other businesses are doing and copy that. The downside to that is you don't know if they are copying someone else and if what they are doing is really working. Why? Most businesses don't really know how to track their results. So they don't know what really works or didn't or if what works cost too much to get the lead or sale.

The second choice is to look up and see what big companies are doing and try to copy that. Of course the downside is, most small businesses don't have enough money or resources to do market that way. Especially when they found out it doesn't get any new leads or sales. Think about the

"Goodyear" blimp at the superbowl each year. How in the world would you measure (if there is anything to measure) responses from a blimp flying around overhead?

Here's what I think is the best answer: Look for direct marketers who know what they are doing. That is they know if the spend $1 they are going to get a return of at least $1. You can find out all about how to do that at my resource: http://businessprofitsacademy.com

If you need a short course on direct marketing get this resource:
"No B.S. Direct Marketing, The Ultimate No Holds Barred Kick Butt Take No Prisoners Direct Marketing for Non-Direct Marketing Businesses, Second Edition" By Dan Kennedy. You can find it at: http://nobsbooks.com

10

Now Grow Your Business
With Street Smarts

Now that you've got some street smarts about marketing you business it's time to roll up your sleeves and go to work. Now I'm not talking about you doing all the work, that's working "in" your business. I'm talking about working "on" your business. You need to know and recognize the difference.

I'm going to use four questions to help you create a map of how to grow your business. My suggestion would be to literally create some kind of visible map. It can be as simple or as elaborate as you want. Just be careful not to spend all your energy creating the map! The importance of the map is to have visible representation that others can easily see and follow and to be a reminder that the process of growing your business is a journey.

Question #1: Who Are You?

Here's the first question: "Who are you?" Creating a profile of who you are as a person is important. What's your personality type? Knowing your behavioral tendencies in your area of strength and liabilities helps you determine how you can approach your business. You can find out more at: http://deanrenfro.com/disc Another helpful tool would be to use "Strength

Finder" to learn your top talent strengths. You can learn more about that at: http://strengthtest.com Another great personality tool can be found at http://howtofascinate.com Sally Hogshead is the designer of this idea and it's a great tool with great graphic. All of these tools will help you gain a clearer picture of who you are and your role in your business.

If you have employees (paid or non-paid) I would suggest you do the same for them. The more you know about who you are working with and what and how they function the easier it will be to put the right people in the right place doing the right thing. This alone can make a huge difference in the success of your business.

The next component of "Who are you?" has to do with the business itself. You must create a clear identity about who and what your business is about. Many small businesses mistakenly think they are in "X" business only to discover they are really in the "Y" business. An example of that might be a plumber who thinks he is in the "plumbing" business repairing burst pipes, installing water heaters and faucet sinks, etc. When in reality he is in the "Emergency Repair" business, solving people's emergency needs. The whole marketing strategy to each one of those is totally different. Not counting the huge expense and disappointment that might come from a marketing campaign that received little or no results. You see this all the time in "ValuPak" coupon mailings all the time.

Question #2 – What's the Destination?

Many times the destination question for businesses is very vague. Not much thought is given to what the business will look like in 5-10 years. Many times a small business grows organically and then discovers the systems in place are stunting and holding back the growth and profitability of the business. If this occurs long enough the business will soon be a descent and eventually die. Almost without fail every small business owner aspires to reach that magical $1million dollar mark in either sales or net profit. But so many factors go into being able to achieve that are overlooked.

How the business is structured, profit margins, price elasticity, customer buying habits, product availability, business location, and numerous other issues can create unseen roadblocks to the desired destination. Knowing how to reach your destination is must be mapped out with specific steps and strategies. Dan Kennedy points out that strategy must precede the tactical aspect of the plan. So many business owners wake up every day and do the same thing they did yesterday (tactical) and expect somehow to arrive at the magical destination (insanity!). Don't fret however! I've mapped out a plan for you to achieve that $1 million dollar or more destination. You can find out about it at: http://businessprofitsacademy.com

Question #3 – How Do I Get There?

Once you have some sense of destination the next logical question is, "how are you going to arrive there?" Most people need some sort of visual guide. My suggestion is to create a road map using a whiteboard and sticky notes (Post-it Notes). The key to this process in the early stages is to write out as many of the component pieces as you can on the sticky notes without trying to arrange them in any order. This allows your mind freedom and thoughts and ideas will come easier than if you try to think through it in some sequential order. (If you are a sequential thinker and that's the best way for you, then do it that way, its okay.) This process may take weeks as you map out all the steps necessary to arrive at your destination. The great thing about the sticky notes – you can reposition them! Once you have some form of flow for your business you can then start using the whiteboard for creating a more organized structure. You can write headings or create boxes or circles and design your own road map.

If you want to do all of this in some digital format you can you any one of the "mind mapping" tools out there as well. I just find that if you do all the hands on writing and physical rearranging of the task, ideas and processes it comes easier for most people. For me the mind map tool becomes the final step, once you have worked through all the data, ideas, and process and are clear about the destination you then can create a "pretty" document with the mind map tool.

Question #4 – What Will It Take?

The fourth question is, "What will it take to get to my destination?" Many times small business owners jump in and just start doing business. I applaud that! Getting started is huge. I think it was Einstein that said, "a body in motion tends to stay in motion." A small business owner has to also grasp that "every action has an equal and opposite reaction." Knowing how you are going to fund your business, knowing what price point it takes to make the profit you need to grow your business. Knowing how much it cost to acquire a customer and then keep a customer. Knowing what is the best business model for your business, because different models produce different results the further you go down the road.

What kind of legal and financial structure are you going to create for your business? Seeking professional guidance in this area is very important. But if you haven't mapped out where you are going you could very well create a roadblock for your business down the road. Being able to see how you could ramp up your business to the next level – whether that's in production, sales, employees could be vital to the extended existence of your business. So often small businesses are built on the owner's personality, style or drive. Believe me, those are important. But, many times that is not reproducible! And if you can't reproduce it, you usually can't expand it.

It's not the intent of this book to exhaust these four questions. That's another book in and of itself! But, thinking through this question is vital to your business. Street Smart business owners are always asking questions. They are always adapting. So where do you go from here? Great question! Let's see ....

So What Do You Do From Here?

One last kick in the seat of the pants – Take Action! Massive action! If you are still sitting on your laurels or your butt, send me an email or give me a call – you need a swift kick! One of the biggest barriers to making a profit, creating more leads, growing your business is procrastination! Whatever your reason, excuse, condition or laziness, get up and get busy. Get Started. One of my most favorite quotes is, "if you always do, what you have always done, you will always get what you have right now! How's that working for ya?" Another one is, "A body in motion, tends to stay in motion."

I know everything is not perfect, not everything is exactly figured out, not everything is a sure bet, not everything is going to be fun! But you need to get started. If you need to reread the book, then do it. If you need to talk to a professional, then do it! If you need to generate some more leads, then do it. If you need to change your business practices, then do it! If you need to change personnel, then do it! If you need resources, then do it!

Here's what you need to know - the game of business is won by those who go and do it! Not the ones on the sideline sitting on their behinds! If you need a new skill, go learn it. If you need a new supplier with a better profit margin, then find one! If you need a new routine, then start it!

Everything written in this book was learned through trial and error. There is no fluff, no theory, no "hope so" in this book. Will they all work for you? I don't know – but you won't either – until you give them a try!

If you are like most people you need a plan or a model or a system. I've got that solved. I have a whole system of step-by-step street smart strategies that takes you through the process of growing your business, generating more leads, creating more and bigger profits. I've got "done for you" tools and resources that you can just plug and play! So get smart and quit trading hours for dollars and start working on your business not just in your business.

So here's what you need to do:

1. **Change!** Realize that if you don't change the way you are doing business (or not) – you'll stay broke and probably lose your business, your health and maybe your family! (Statistics bear this out)

2. **Implement a system.** All throughout this book I have recommended resources for you. The main one is my online business academy. Go test it out. See for yourself. Are you a brand new business startup? Go to http://bizstartupacademy.com Sign up and get in my system.
   It's FREE to sign up! If you are an existing business then go to http://businessprofitsacademy.com and sign up. It's FREE to sign up and you'll learn a lot.

3. **Get a coach.** Every successful athlete and business person has a coach. A coach will give you an outside perspective. He or she will see what you can't or are not willing to see and give you different options. A coach will hold you accountable to what you said you would or wouldn't

do. All I can tell you from personal experience is, "If you want to go to the next level, a coach is necessary."

Last thing - If you are already an accomplished business owner and earning in excess of $250,000.00 per year (rich according to some folk at the Federal Government) use this book as directions to enhance the speed of your business success and then find someone to coach or mentor.